C000280398

The discovery of the springs

▲ Ben Satchwell (1732–1810), Leamington's first postmaster. Satchwell, together with William Abbotts, discovered Leamington's second saline spring.

▲ All Saints' Church and old cottages, 1822.

The original spring lay on the Earl of Aylesford's property south of the river Leam. A well house, known as 'Lord Aylesford's Well', was first built over the spring in 1804. Commercial exploitation of the spring was stopped by Aylesford, who wished to keep it freely accessible for everybody.

Local businessmen William Abbotts and Ben Satchwell were eager to discover a second spring to attract visitors to the town and make their fortunes. In 1784 the two men discovered a salty spring bubbling up in a pool of water on Abbotts' land, west of Lord Aylesford's Well. Abbotts sunk a well on the spot and in 1788 opened Leamington's first proper bathhouse.

Ever 'spr six so river Leam. Each gave rise to a bathhouse, including the Royal Pump Rooms.

Lord Aylesford's Well in about 1815. ▼

From handpumps to horsepower

In the 1890s, water from Lord Aylesford's Well – Leamington's original spring – could be *'taken free in small quantities from the pump erected outside the building, wine bottles filled for 1d each.'*

The photograph was probably taken about 1890, shortly before the shops blocking the view to the church were demolished.

The Well House itself was demolished in 1960. ▼

In Leamington there was no shortage of spring water for both drinking and bathing – its greatest advantage over rivals Cheltenham and Bath. One 19th century guide to Leamington spoke scathingly of Cheltenham's *'slow and scanty'* saline spring and the town's habit of *'constructing baths…and filling them with common water'*.

Spa water bubbled up from the ground naturally at Leamington's original spring. As demand grew, new wells had to be dug so that the spa water could be pumped up in large quantities. At first water was pumped up by hand.

Then some baths used horses to operate their pumps, later replacing them with steam engines. A two-horsepower steam engine installed in the newly opened Royal Pump Rooms in 1814 was proudly described by James Bisset as able to *'force up as many tons of the Mineral Fluid in a few hours, as would fairly float a British Man of War!'*

More and more visitors came to Leamington, paying to drink the waters and take a bath in the growing number of spa establishments. To accommodate the visitors, new streets were laid out in the Old Town. Speculators and investors built elegant terraces such as Charlotte Street, as well as luxurious hotels like the Copps' Royal Hotel.

The expanding town also spread north of the river Leam, where from 1808 a New Town was developed on land owned by Mr Bertie Greatheed. To succeed, the New Town needed a new bath house that lay closer than the baths south of the river Leam. Despite extensive searching at the northern end of The Parade, no saline water could be found – the sandstone here carries only fresh water.

At last, in 1811, a spring was discovered just north of the river, between the Old and New Towns. This became the site for 'The Royal Baths and Pump Room', now more usually known as the Royal Pump Rooms.

▲ Copps' Royal Hotel on the corner of High Street and Clemens Street. This was opened in 1827 and demolished in 1847 to make way for the new railway bridge.

'Taste and Simple Elegance'

The Royal Pump Rooms was designed by Warwick architect C S Smith and built *'on a grand scale'* at a reputed cost of £25,000. The 20 baths (17 hot and three cold) had separate areas for ladies and gentlemen, entered from opposite ends of the building. The new baths opened in July 1814 and quickly became established as the most prestigious in Leamington.

'Let Strangers, who have roam'd these Isles, Or those who foreign climes have scann'd, Say if in It'ly, France, or Spain, They e'er saw PUBLIC BATHS so grand? Or if a PUMP ROOM can be found To equal this on British ground?'
(James Bisset, 1816)

◄ The Royal Pump Rooms included a bath chair, *'which is an excellent contrivance for the safe and easy conveyance of the bather from the undressing chair into the bath'*. A bath chair can be seen by the colonnade in this print of 1843.

Royal recognition

▲ Queen Victoria as a young woman.

Queen Victoria first visited Leamington in 1830 when she was an 11 year old princess. In 1838, a year after Victoria became Queen, a formal application for a new title for the town was made. The young Queen was *'graciously pleased'* to grant a Charter allowing the town to adopt the name 'Royal Leamington Spa'.

Major Abiathar Hawkes, the town's Master of Ceremonies, was the driving force behind gaining the Royal Charter. Leamington was facing a financial disaster in 1838 and many buildings in the New Town were unfinished. People hoped that the prestigious new name would attract more visitors to take the waters.

▲ Major Abiathar Hawkes (1786–1861), one of the deputation of three who in 1838 successfully petitioned Queen Victoria for the privilege of styling the town 'Royal Leamington Spa'.

Leamington Old Town in the early 1840s. This panoramic view shows that the humble village of 301 inhabitants in 1801 had become a major inland resort, with a population of 12,812 in 1841. ▼

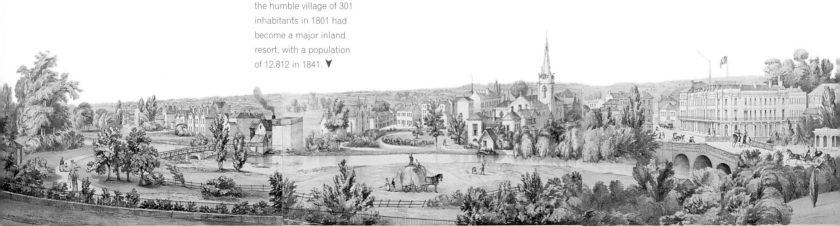

The rapid development of Britain's transport systems in the 19th century at first promoted the rise of Leamington as a fashionable spa resort, then led to its eclipse by seaside and continental resorts.

The development of a network of stagecoach services in the early 19th century made it much easier for high society to travel to inland resorts like Leamington. However the subsequent construction of the railway network from the 1840s meant Leamington, and its rivals Bath and Cheltenham, faced growing competition from seaside resorts and continental spas.

During the second half of the 19th century high society gradually stopped coming to Leamington to take the waters. Leamington slowly became a residential town rather than a fashionable spa. Many ex-colonial civil servants, Army and Navy officers came to Leamington to retire, attracted by the large houses, now cheap to buy or rent, and the number of available domestic servants.

▲ By the 1820s stage-coaches ran regularly between Leamington and towns such as Coventry, London and Birmingham. This painting, showing a coach leaving an inn, is one of a series by James and George Temple.

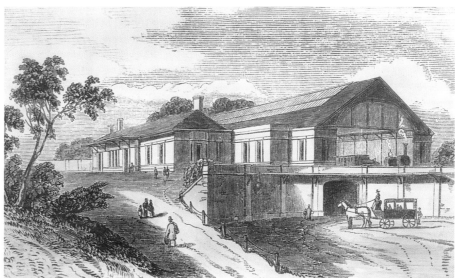

◄ In 1844 the first railway station opened in Leamington, soon leading to the replacement of the horse drawn stage-coaches. In 1852 the Great Western Railway linked the town directly to London.

This picture shows Leamington Station in that year. Although the railway greatly improved communications, its stations, track and bridges blighted the centre of the Old Town.

Medicine men

'Leamington is in a great degree supported by a class of persons who live upon their private fortunes and seek the place either for health, recreation or comfort. Health and cleanliness are the staple commodities which Leamington has to sell.'
(Public Health Report, 1850)

In a spa town where people came for the benefit of their health, doctors were among the most important residents. Dr Amos Middleton encouraged visitors to come to the spa and published general rules for taking the waters. The treatments he prescribed were the standard until Dr Henry Jephson came to Leamington.

Dr Jephson began practising in the town in 1823. He believed strongly in the powers of the saline waters and set out new rules for drinking and bathing. People from the highest levels of society consulted him, increasing the popularity of the spa. Dr John Hitchman came to Leamington in 1840 and set up practice in Clemens Street. All three doctors practiced as surgeons or physicians in the Warneford Hospital, which opened in 1832.

▲ Dr Henry Jephson (1798–1878) in later life.

The Warneford Hospital. ➤

TAKING THE WATERS

The season for taking the waters lasted from May to October. Patients were advised to stay at least a month, drinking the spa waters and bathing in them two or three times a week. Patients were instructed to drink a pint (about half a litre) of the 'nauseous' tasting water in the morning, followed by a walk and breakfast. Dr Jephson was very specific about the diet he prescribed: it included plain meat, stale bread, plain puddings, sherry, black tea and butter – and no fruit or vegetables!

The spa treatments were largely for the wealthy but some provision was made for the poor. Dr Jephson offered free treatment to the needy in the early morning, three baths were set aside for use by the poor in the Royal Pump Rooms, and free spa water was available from a basin outside Aylesford's Well. The Warneford Hospital also offered free baths to the poor.

'At early dawn prepare to rise,
And if your health you really prize,
To drink the WATERS quick repair,
Then take a walk to breathe fresh air,
Hie thro' the fields – or promenade
Round Pump Rooms grand, or Colonnade.

A second glass now take – what then?
Why! Take a pleasant walk again,
The WATERS, exercise, and air,
Will brace your nerves, your health repair.

Then to your breakfast haste away,
With what keen appetite you may.'

(James Bisset, 1816)

Three types of water were available for treatments at different establishments in the town: saline (salty), sulphurous and chalybeate (containing iron). Spa waters were said to cure all sorts of illness, from rheumatism to stomach problems. The spa waters tasted horrible – yellowish green and smelly sulphurous water – and were mildly laxative!

▲ James Bisset (1760–1832), a Scot who became a businessman in Birmingham, moved to Leamington in 1811. Here he opened a Museum of Curiosities and a Picture Gallery and Reading Room. He also wrote a Guide Book and verse promoting the new spa resort and its attractions.

CONTENTS OF AN IMPERIAL PINT OF EACH OF THE LEAMINGTON MINERAL WATERS.

SPRINGS.	GASES, IN CUBIC INCHES.				SALTS, IN GRAINS.						Total of the Salts in Grains
	Oxygen	Azote	Carbonic Acid	Sulphuretted Hydrogen	Sulphate of Soda	Chloride of Sodium	Chloride of Calcium	Chloride of Magnesium	Silica	Peroxide of Iron	
Lord Aylesford's	.075	.537	2.103	none	40.398	40.770	20.561	3.266	none	a trace	105.093
Mr. Smith's	.015	.658	2.503	none	40.234	47.865	19.772	2.121	none	a trace	109.992
Mr. Wise's	.088	.488	2.180	none	39.157	26.610	18.737	22.592	none	a trace	107.396
Mr. Robbins'	.075	.538	2.356	none	28.619	35.350	23.511	8.468	none	a trace	95.948
Mr. Reid's { Sulphureous	.025	.725	3.156	1.141	28.065	25.605	15.777	9.695	none	a trace	79.142
Saline	.025	.565	2.162	none	30.610	42.922	17.987	10.813	0.972	0.265	103.575
Imperial Fount. { Chalybeate	.075	.645	3.294	none	34.294	55.271	25.059	3.927	8.580	8.580	135.711
Saline	.098	.763	3.156	none	34.435	14.534	17.570	26.050	none	a trace	92.589
Sulphureous	.012	.612	3.531	1.142	31.112	7.301	39.305	19.494	3.620	0.530	101.362
Royal { Sulphureous	.064	.498	3.156	1.140	5.546	5.140	3.365	1.156	none	a trace	15.211
Pump Room { Saline	.066	.588	2.950	none	32.744	67.782	20.902	12.363	1.045	0.956	135.792

◄ This table from a Guide Book published in1833 shows the contents of the seven main springs.

Visitors welcome

▲ The Duke of Wellington, conqueror of Napoleon Bonaparte at the battle of Waterloo, stayed in Leamington in 1827.

The fashionable spa resort of Leamington attracted royalty, politicians, artists, literary figures and rich eccentrics. Visitors included the Prince Regent, Queen Adelaide, the Crown Prince and Princess of Denmark, the famous architect John Nash, the violinist and composer Paganini, and the art critic and social reformer John Ruskin.

Author Nathaniel Hawthorne stayed in Leamington for a few months and Charles Dickens set one of his scenes in 'Dombey and Son' in Holly Walk. Many of Leamington's streets were named in honour of its famous residents and visitors – Augusta Place is named after the Prince Regent's sister and Eastnor Grove after Lord Eastnor.

The Regent Hotel, which opened in 1819, was one of the largest hotels in Europe. It was reputed to have had 100 bedrooms – but only one bathroom! ▼

Leamington was popular with fortune hunters in the 19th century – 'gentlemen' were drawn to the town because of the many rich heiresses living in the spa. Equally, mothers with marriageable daughters also set eyes on prosperous male visitors arriving in town!

'At Leamington, unquestionably, no dross of society, or even ambiguous characters, will be found among those who assemble at the Pumproom for their health and the waters. The place is yet too choice and too costly to admit of any but the very tip top of society.'

(Dr A B Granville, 1841)

The Upper Assembly Rooms in the New Town, built in 1812, housed a ballroom, reading room, card room, billiard room and refectory. Wealthy people came to the Assembly Rooms for the programme of concerts, balls and dramatic performances. This shows a Musical Festival in October 1833. The Old Town had its own Assembly Rooms, opened in 1821 and offering a similar range of pleasures. ➤

Masters of Ceremonies like Major Abiathar Hawkes were very influential. They organised social events to entertain the town's wealthy and famous guests. Visitors did not come only for treatments – *'taking the waters'* was often an excuse to join stylish society.

The elite gathered beneath the *'glittering chandeliers'* of the Assembly Rooms for concerts, balls, card games and plays. Theatres, libraries and museums were equally popular. The Master of Ceremonies' task was to keep the visitors entertained – and to guarantee acceptable social behaviour. He set out detailed dress codes and rules for specific occasions, to ensure the town's fashionable visitors were not upset by uncouth manners!

▲ Napoleon Bonaparte's nephew Prince Charles Louis Napoleon (later Napoleon III), while in exile from France, stayed in Leamington during 1838–39. He was a keen sportsman and much sought as a guest for parties and receptions.

For richer...fashionable façades

'The inhabitants of the principal streets and squares I believe enjoy a higher state of health than in most towns.'

(Mr Watson, medical officer for the Leamington District, 1849)

By the 1820s housing in the Old Town was considered unfashionable. Wealthy residents lived in majestic Regency houses in the New Town. Instead of having plain brick fronts like the earlier Georgian houses, the buildings in the New Town were often finished in stucco (a type of render). The stucco was coloured to resemble natural stone, imitating the fashionable stone buildings of Bath.

The trend to paint the stuccoed fronts in pastel colours – the way we see the façades today – dates from the late 19th century. The Parade, Euston Place, Waterloo Place and Clarendon Square, lined with big houses, were amongst the fashionable addresses in Leamington.

Terraces of fine houses and shops on the lower Parade and Euston Place in about 1850. The Royal Pump Rooms, with its fenced garden, can be seen in the background. ▼

▲ Labourers working on the
wall of All Saints' Church.

Poor people were drawn to Leamington to work on the construction sites in the New Town or found employment in the service industries, cooking and cleaning for the wealthy visitors and residents. Later, jobs were available with the iron foundries, breweries and carriage-builders.

Life for the poor was hard. Many were badly nourished and poorly clothed, often working six days a week for low wages.

Children had to leave school at an early age to help support the family, sometimes becoming errand boys or chimney sweeps.

Hidden behind the tall Regency buildings were narrow, squalid streets and courts offering poorly built housing for the working classes. The small houses were often damp and overcrowded, with up to nine people sharing a house with only one bedroom.

In the unpaved yards behind the houses were pumps supplying drinking water, right next to cesspits, pigsties and privies (toilets). The link between this insanitary environment and ill-health amongst the poor was evident to medical inspectors such as Mr Watson, who *'found diarrhoea and fever more frequently to prevail where nuisances exist'*.

'The condition of the poor is so defective, that in their present state, it is almost impossible to rid them of the nuisances...that I have frequently observed.'

(Mr Watson, medical officer for the Leamington District, 1849)

◄ Poor conditions for the working classes survived World War II. Leamington's Development Plan published in 1947 comments of Althorpe Street: *'To live in these surroundings cannot produce good citizens or healthy children.'*

Drinking water: kill or cure?

Although water was the key to Leamington's dramatic growth as a health spa, local supplies could be surprisingly poor. In 1841 Dr A B Granville, a fashionable London doctor, suspected that the spa waters in the Royal Pump Rooms were polluted by the river Leam. The quality of drinking water was generally poor and a cholera outbreak in summer 1849 threatened Leamington's reputation as a place for *'taking the waters'*.

The adoption of the Public Health Act of 1848 brought improvements but clean drinking water was not generally available for another 30 years. Henry Bright, later Mayor of Leamington, began his campaign to improve the town's drinking water in 1870. He suggested boring for water instead of filtering it from the River Leam.

Opponents feared this new technique, claiming wrongly that it would damage the saline water supplies. Water was eventually provided by boring and pumping it up. It was some time before it was generally accepted that good quality drinking water and sewerage systems were essential for the health of local residents and visitors.

▲ Alderman Henry Bright's *'untiring exertions'* in providing Leamington with *'pure water'* were commemorated with a drinking fountain and obelisk, placed on Holly Walk in 1880. He also proposed installing a more effective town drainage system.

CHOLERA

Cholera, an infection giving stomach cramps and diarrhoea, is usually fatal unless treated with modern medicines. It is caused by drinking water or eating food contaminated with the bacterium Vibrio comma.

'The rain fell to the river, the sewage to the land.'
A picturesque Leamington saying!

◄ For much of the 19th century Leamington's supply of drinking water came from wells or the river Leam. The river water, which was drawn near the mill at the back of All Saints' Church, was often polluted.

This painting by Frederick Whitehead (1853–1938), shows the river immediately downstream from the mill.

Good quality drinking water was not generally available until the water works (opened in 1879) began to supply from a borehole.

▲ All Saints' Church about 1820. The Royal Pump Rooms can be seen in the background. The church was remodelled and extended several times during the 19th and early 20th centuries, not achieving its full extent until the 1920s.

A thriving spa resort like Leamington needed to provide places of worship and education for its fast growing population of residents and visitors. The parish church of All Saints originally served the whole of Leamington. The growth of the town made it necessary to repeatedly enlarge the church during the 19th century, although other churches and chapels were opened as early as 1816.

It was through the Church and the Sunday School movement that basic education was first provided for the poor. In Leamington the first day-school for poorer children was established in 1822 by the Reverend Wise. Schools gave poor pupils religious and 'other valuable' instruction, and tried to protect them from dangers awaiting them in the streets while their parents were at work.

Wealthy parents were able to pay for tuition and sent their children to private schools such as the Leamington College, opened in 1848. It provided an education in mathematics and classical languages for the 'sons of the nobility, clergy and gentry'. The College closed in 1902 as a result of financial difficulties.

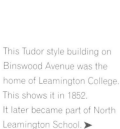

This Tudor style building on Binswood Avenue was the home of Leamington College. This shows it in 1852. It later became part of North Leamington School. ➤

Gardens for all

▲ Edward Willes, of Newbold Comyn, donor of the land used for Jephson Gardens. His generosity to Leamington is commemorated on an obelisk erected in the gardens in 1875.

'Leamington to-day ranks among the most leafy, picturesque and open of English towns'.
(Guide Book, 1918–19)

Parks and gardens played an important part in the development of Leamington, offering leisure activities and contributing to the town's image as 'Leafy Leamington'. As well as providing places in which to walk and play, they were venues for public fêtes, sporting events and entertainments including (during the summer season) orchestras playing on the bandstands. One of the earliest was the Ranelagh Pleasure Gardens, opened in Old Town in 1811. An admission fee was charged to enter the 'tastefully laid out and furnished' gardens.

In 1834 farmland beside the Leam was laid out as pleasure gardens. Two years later the owners of the land, the Willes family of Newbold Comyn Hall, leased these gardens to trustees at a nominal rent, on condition that the ground was never built upon. The gardens were renamed in honour of Dr Henry Jephson in 1846, when lodges were built at the main entrances and, three years later, a statue of Jephson was unveiled. Jephson Gardens were open free of charge on Sunday afternoons, to allow the less fortunate to enjoy the park.

The tradition of illuminating the Jephson Gardens with lights, begun around 1900, was re-introduced between 1951 and 1961 with the 'Lights of Leamington'. Thousands of lamps transformed the gardens into an *'enchanted fairyland'.* ➤

The lodges at The Parade entrance to Jephson Gardens. ▼

▲ Artists painted the rolling hills of Warwickshire and its impressive castles, churches, ruins and stately homes for rich visitors and the local gentry. This painting of the church at Offchurch is by Edwin Toovey (1826–1906).

'It matters little in which direction one turns – there are objects of intense interest, of great natural beauty, of vivid historical or literary association, on every hand.'
(Guide Book, 1918–19)

Dr Jephson and Dr Middleton recommended exercise – especially promenading (leisurely walking). Promenading proved popular because it was a healthy pastime and offered visitors the opportunity to explore Leamington and its surroundings.

Equally important, it gave them a chance 'to be seen' and to show off their fashionable clothes! Jephson Gardens, Wilderness, Lover's Walk, York Walk, Holly Walk – the variety of promisingly named walks were an invitation to explore Leamington.

WARWICK CASTLE
The Seat of the R Hon'ble the Earl of Warwick

◄ Other popular places for promenading close to Leamington included Warwick Castle, Stoneleigh Park, Guy's Cliffe and Offchurch. In this print of 1845, Warwick Castle is being viewed from the bridge over the river Avon.

Playing the game

▲ The inaugural 'Leamington and Midland Counties Archery Meeting' was held in 1851. A great success, the event was held annually for nearly 50 years.

Some people came to Leamington for the waters – and others came for sport! Leamington offered a 'watering season' during the summer and a 'hunting season' in winter. Fashionable visitors attended the Warwickshire Hunt, one of the best in the country. Steeplechasing, polo, archery, croquet and tennis were other favourite pastimes.

Archery – *'stimulating body and soul'* – was popular with both ladies and gentlemen. Lawn tennis was developed in Leamington by Major Harry Gem and his friend Jean Batista Perera, a Spanish merchant who lived in the town. The world's first Lawn Tennis Club was founded in Leamington in 1872 and Lawn Tennis Tournaments were held from 1882 to at least 1913.

'The hunting man…views Leamington as a sort of paradise on earth, as social club life can be enjoyed there, and he can hunt six days a week.'
(Guide Book, 1918–19)

Leamington Grand Steeple Chase, 1837. This coloured engraving names the riders, who include the Marquess of Waterford and Captain Beecher. ▼

▲ The main Assembly Room being used as a tea room in about 1920. The room has changed relatively little since the redevelopment of 1862–63, when ground floor widows were added and a wall knocked through to create an alcove where spa water was served.

From the 1840s, as the fashion for visiting inland spa resorts started to decline, Leamington's spa baths began to close. Even the prestigious Royal Pump Rooms was affected, so in 1861 it was sold to a new company made up of influential townspeople led by Dr Jephson.

The south annexe was added in 1910 as a lounge and reading room. ▼

The new company employed local architect John Cundall to renovate the building. In 1862–63 he rebuilt the roof, adding a tower and pediment, and spaced out the colonnade pillars. He also added 'a superior swimming pool' and a Turkish Bath. Despite the new services the Royal Pump Rooms made losses and was purchased by the Local Board of Health in 1868.

In 1875 the new Leamington Corporation took control of the building, carrying out further improvements designed by William de Normanville in 1885–90, including adding a second swimming pool. About 1950 the tower and pediment were removed.

The simpler lines of the Royal Pump Rooms following the alterations of about 1950 can be seen in this travel poster. ▼

Royal **LEAMINGTON SPA**

TRAVEL BY TRAIN WESTERN REGION

The Turkish Bath and 'Ladies Pool'

▲ The 'Ladies' Pool'.

The Turkish Bath in the Royal Pump Rooms was originally four rooms, with separate waiting and changing rooms for ladies and gentlemen. The large 'hammam' was the 'frigidarium' or cooling room. The small room next door was the 'tepidarium', one of the hot rooms (in the hottest room the temperature could rise to 93°C!).

In the mid-1970s so few people used the bath that it was closed and the cooling room used as the physiotherapists' staff room. The pool added to the Royal Pump Rooms in 1863 was used on alternate days by men and women until 1890. After this the new larger pool was used by men and the smaller pool was reserved for women and children, becoming known as the 'Ladies' Pool'.

As part of the redevelopment of the Royal Pump Rooms in 1997–99 (see page 23), the Turkish Bath was converted into a Local History Gallery and the 'Ladies' Pool' became an Art Gallery.

The 'hammam' or cooling room of the Turkish Bath after restoration in 1997–99. It now forms part of a Local History Gallery. ▼

About 1950 the 'Ladies' Pool' was part filled-in and a ramp installed to create a pool for physiotherapy treatments. The new National Health Service used it to treat patients with rheumatism and polio – the buoyancy of the saline spa water helped to support them during exercises. This shows young polio patients receiving treatment. ➤

▲ The swimming pool of 1890, designed by William de Normanville, with its innovative iron roof structure. This photograph shows the pool in the late 1980s.

The unusual roof was refurbished as part of the redevelopment of 1997–99. It now forms a distinctive feature in the public Library which was relocated into the former swimming pool in 1999. ➤

A large new swimming pool was added to the Royal Pump Rooms and opened in 1890. William de Normanville, the borough surveyor who designed the pool, installed in the unique iron roof structure two sprays – these showered water onto the bathers below, cooling the air and giving *'an effect in the sunlight at once pretty and refreshing'*.

In winter the pool was covered with boards and functioned as the 'Winter Hall' for dances and other entertainment. Until about 1950 the larger pool was used by male swimmers, after which it was used by both sexes. In 1990 the pool in the Royal Pump Rooms was closed, following the opening of a new public swimming pool in Newbold Comyn Leisure Centre.

The former swimming pool in the Royal Pump Rooms was converted into a public Library as part of the redevelopment of 1997–99.

Swimming gala in the pool designed by William de Normanville. ▼

The appliance of science

▲ The Vortex pool.
The patient sat on a stool
in warm water aerated with
bubbles, stimulating the
circulation.

Hydrotherapy or water treatments were carried out at the Royal Pump Rooms until 1990. Exercising in warm water built up muscles, soothed joints and eased injuries, and was particularly helpful for arthritis and polio sufferers. Other treatments, such as hot wax applications, steam baths and electrical therapies improved circulation and stimulated muscles.

Many people, including physio-therapists, hydrotherapy assistants, laundresses, and swimming pool and pump room staff looked after those taking Leamington's waters. Meanwhile engineers kept equipment in order and maintained the water in the treatment pool at a steady 97° F (35.5° C).

▲ This Progessive
Treatment Unit produced
ranges of low frequency
electric currents. It was
used to stimulate muscles
and the circulation.

▲ This woman is exper-
iencing a Schnee bath. An
electrical current was passed
through the tubs, stimulating
muscles and improving
circulation in the limbs.

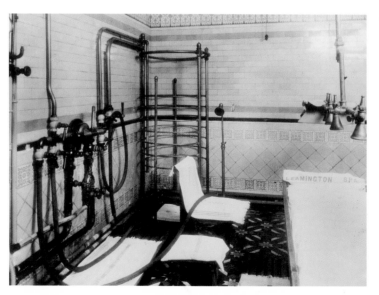

◄ Treatment room
with needle shower.
This sprayed fine, needle-
like jets of water over the
patient from all sides.
The shower was used to
cleanse the skin and
regulate the patient's
skin temperature before
treatment. Patients took
a second needle shower
after their treatment, to
cool them down. They
were then wrapped in warm
towels and allowed to rest
for 20 minutes. The slab
for high pressure shower
('Vichy Douche') treatments
is in the right foreground.